THE LAST OF US
UNOFFICIAL
COLORING BOOK

THE LAST OF US
UNOFFICIAL
COLORING BOOK

Illustrated by
Valentin Ramon

Published by:
Ulysses Press
PO Box 3440
Berkeley, CA 94703
www.ulyssespress.com

ISBN: 978-1-64604-610-2

Printed in the United States
2 4 6 8 10 9 7 5 3 1

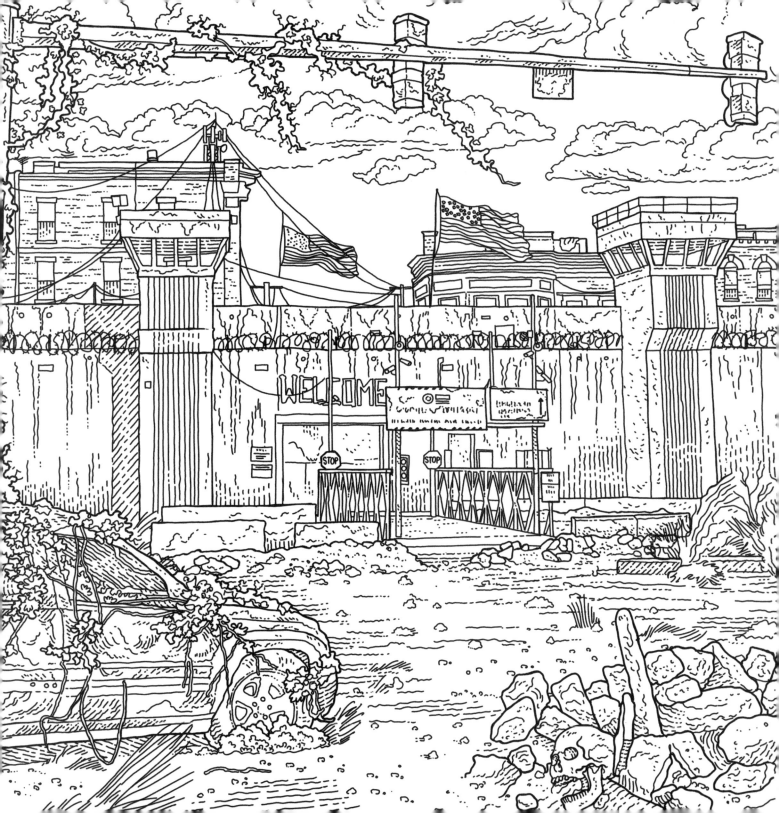

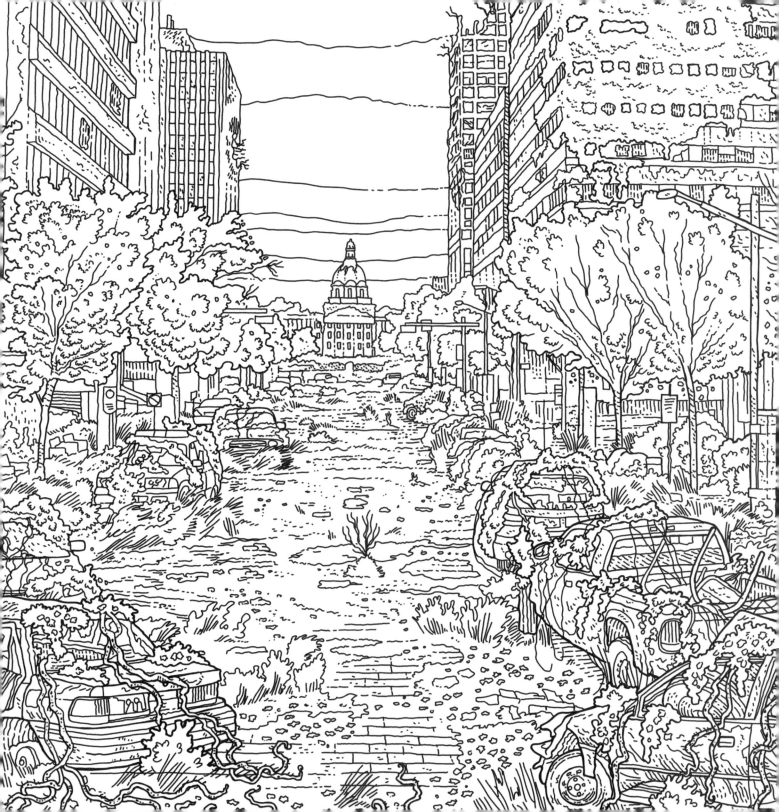

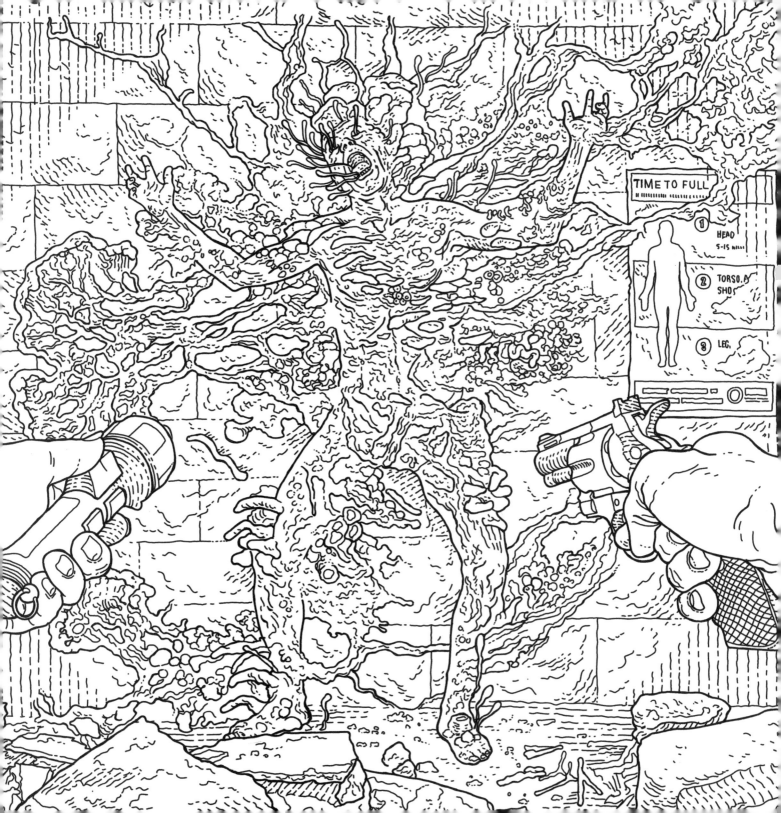

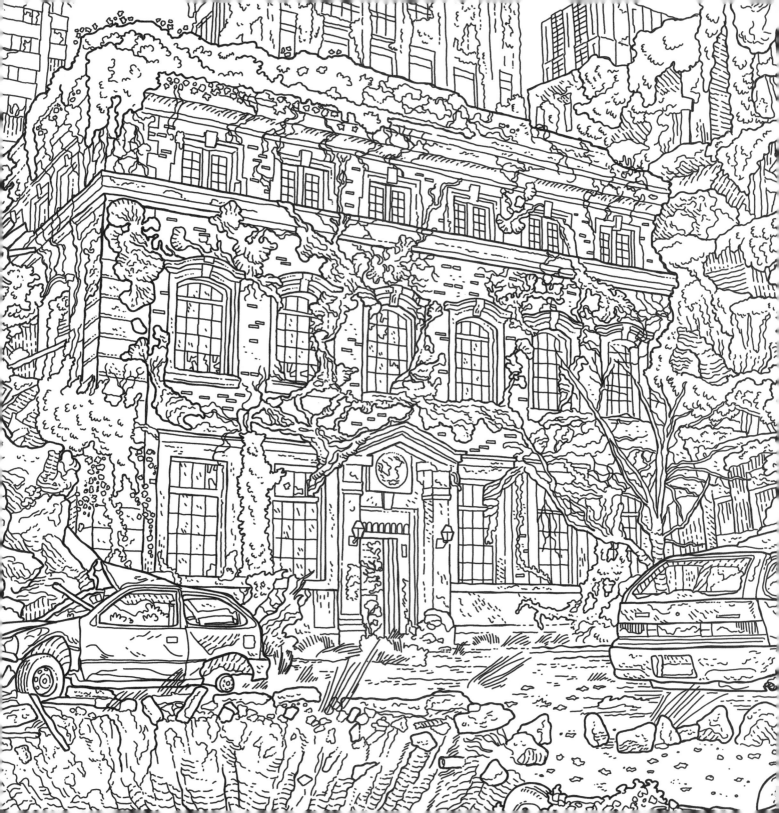

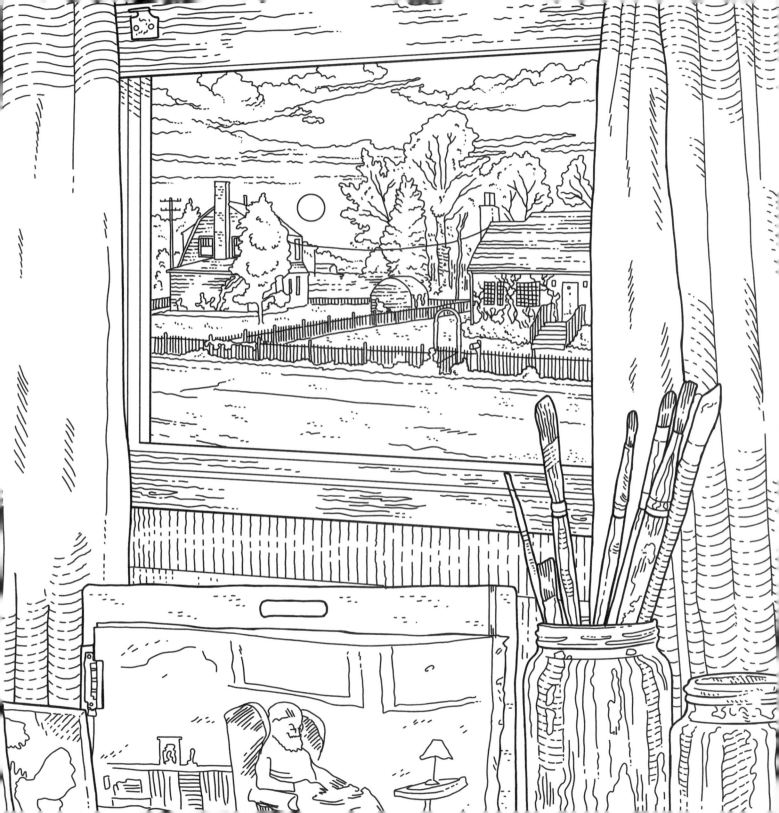

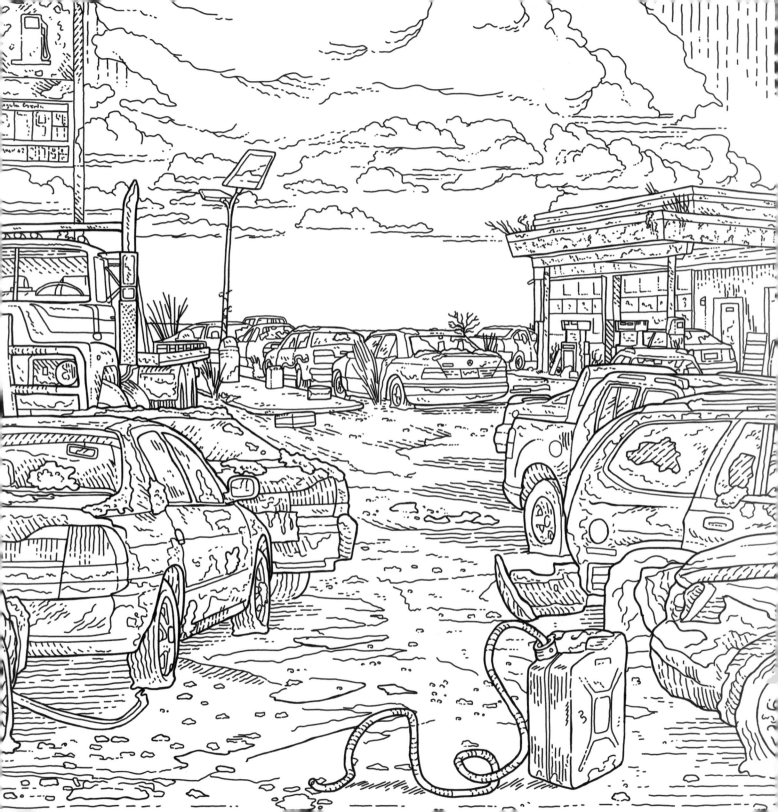

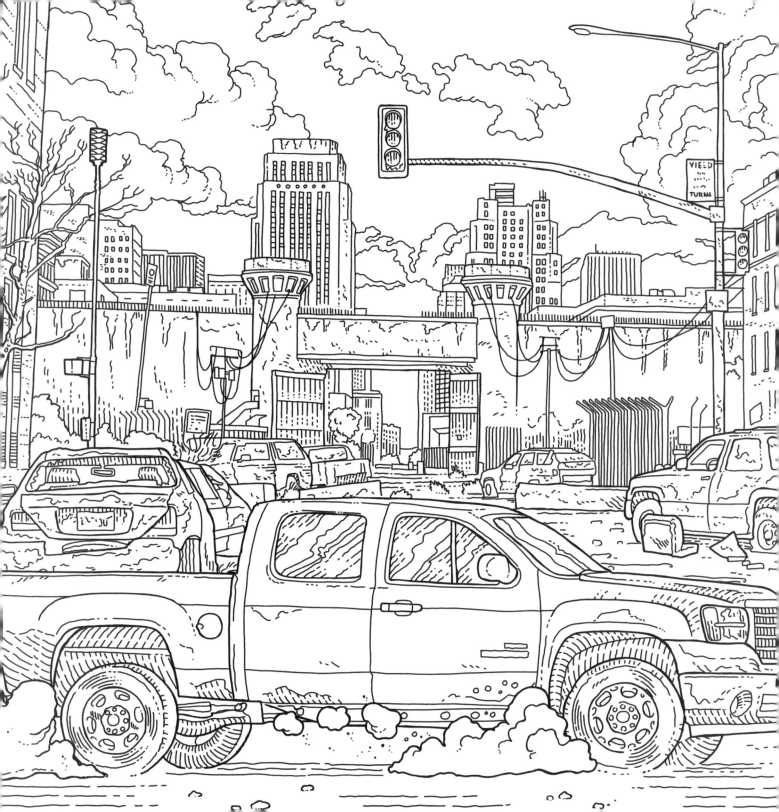

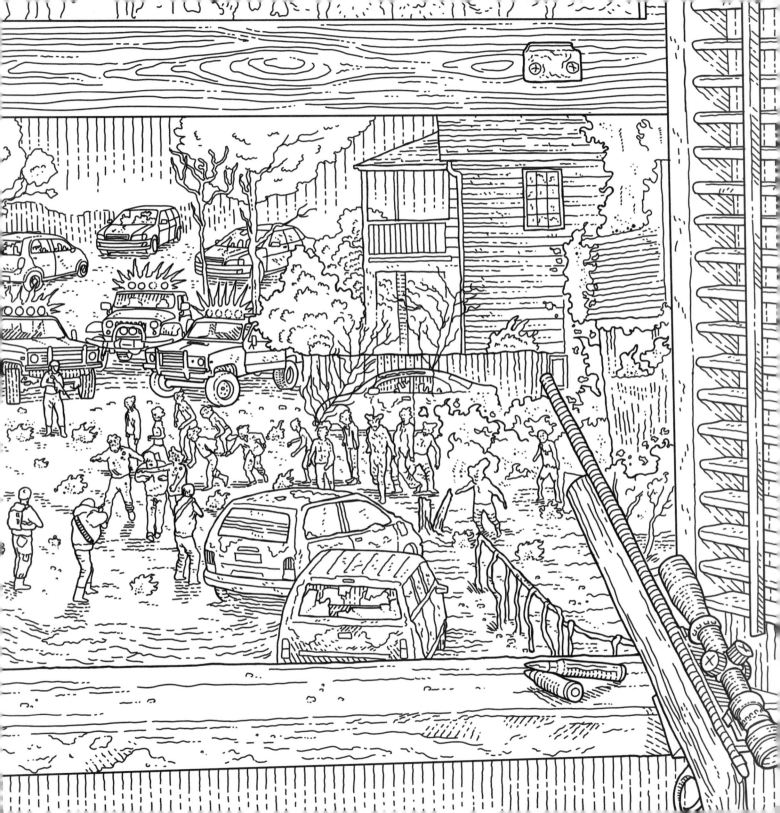

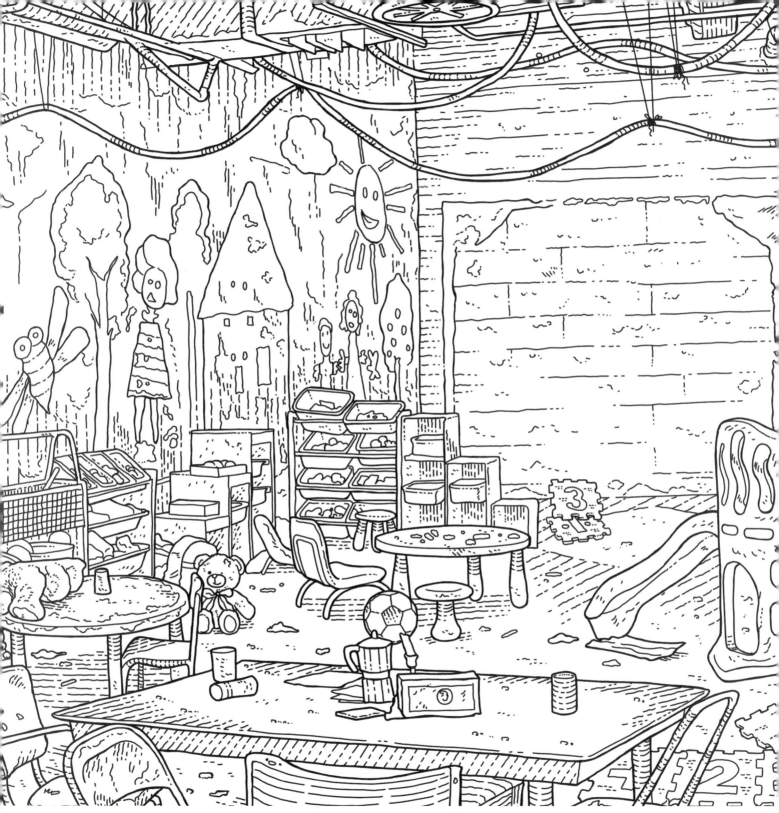

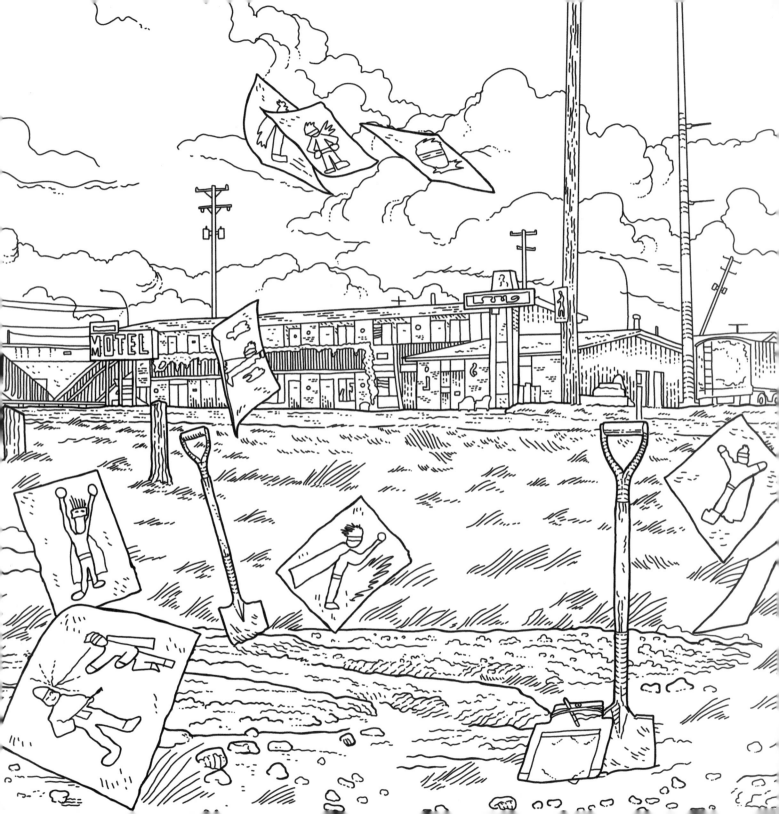

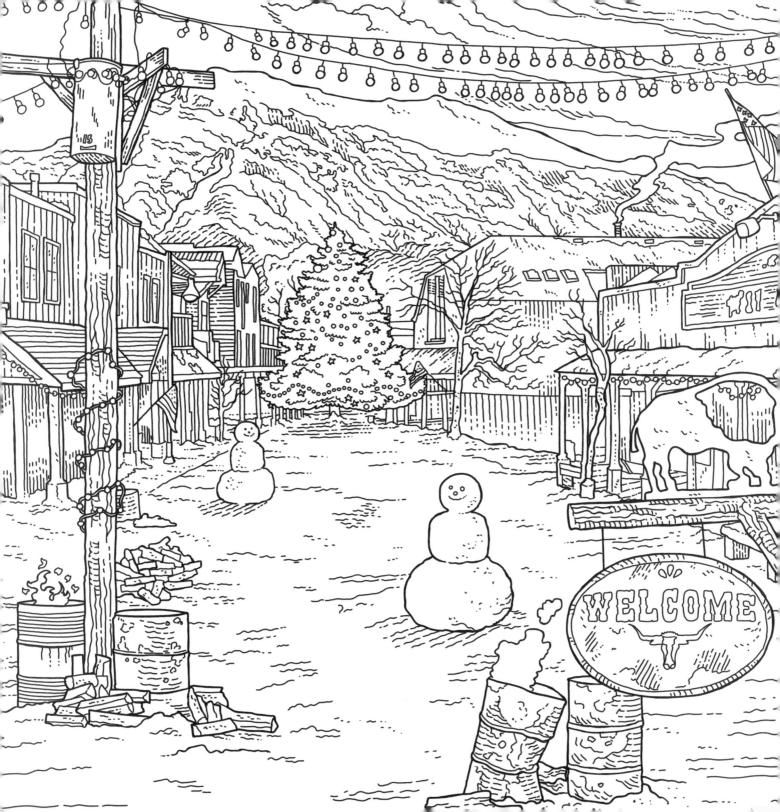

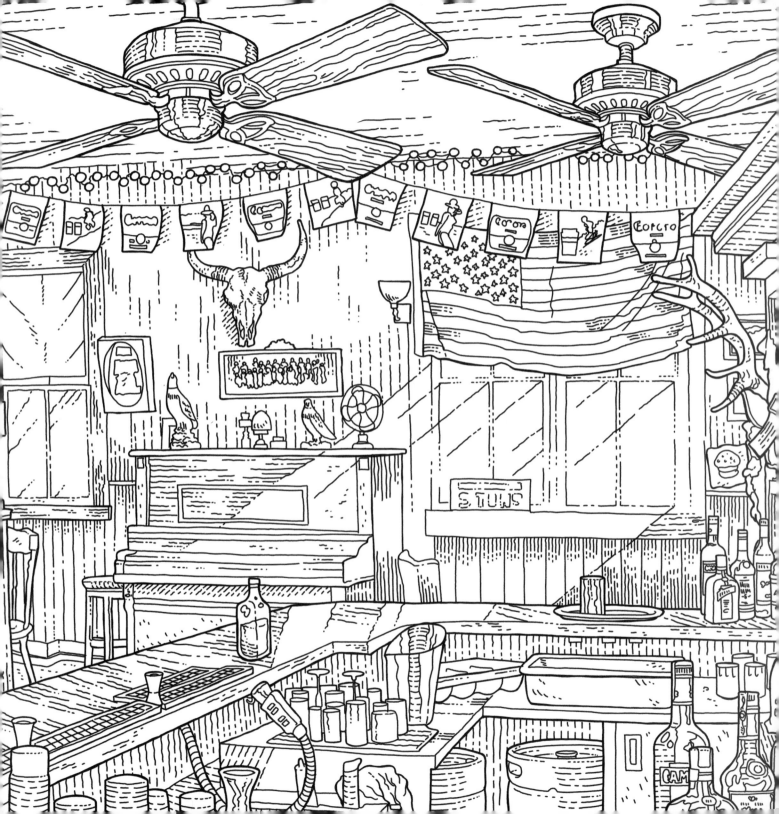

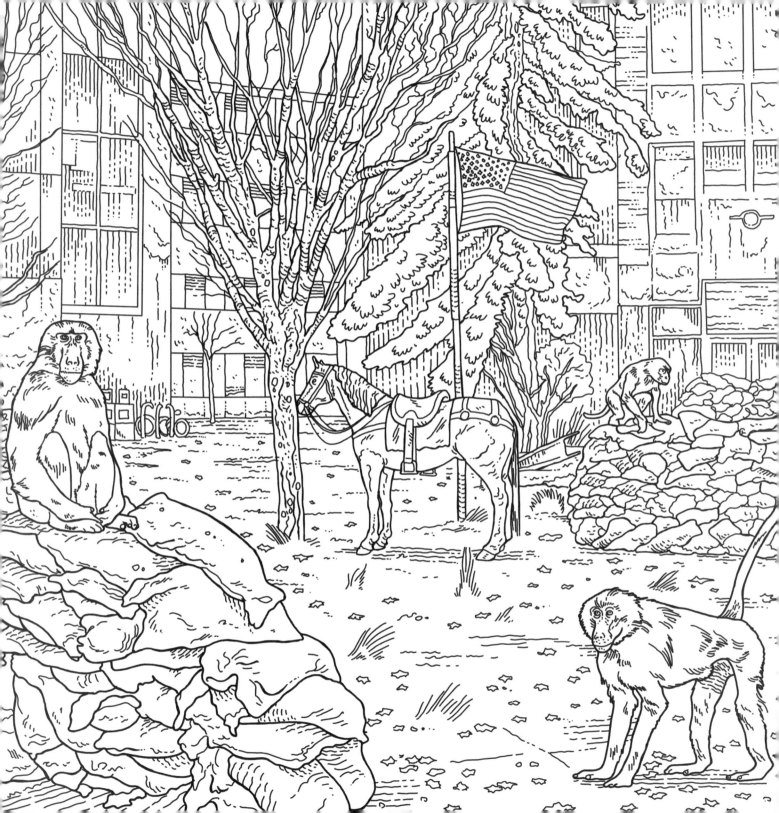

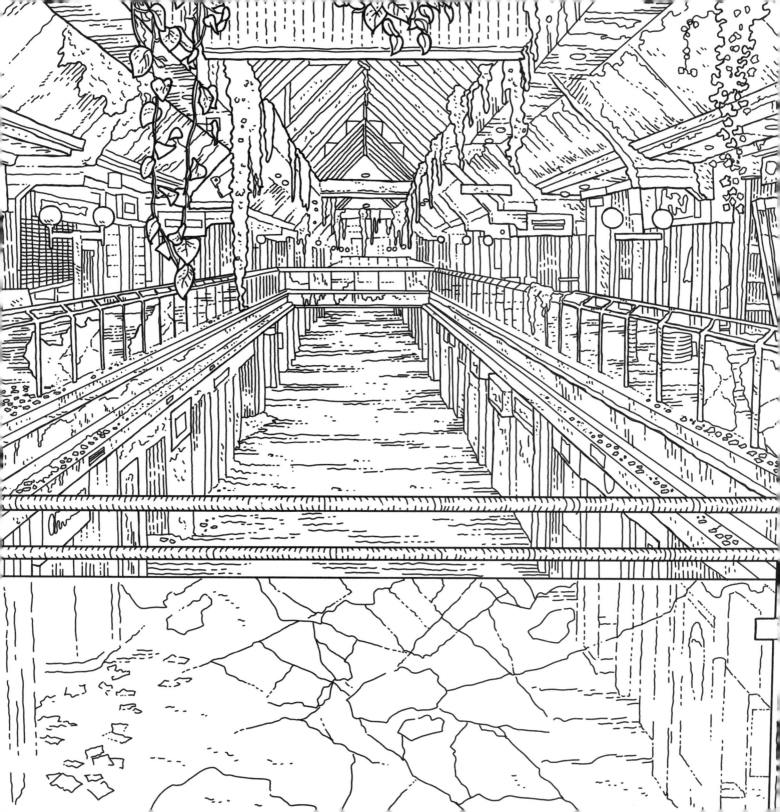

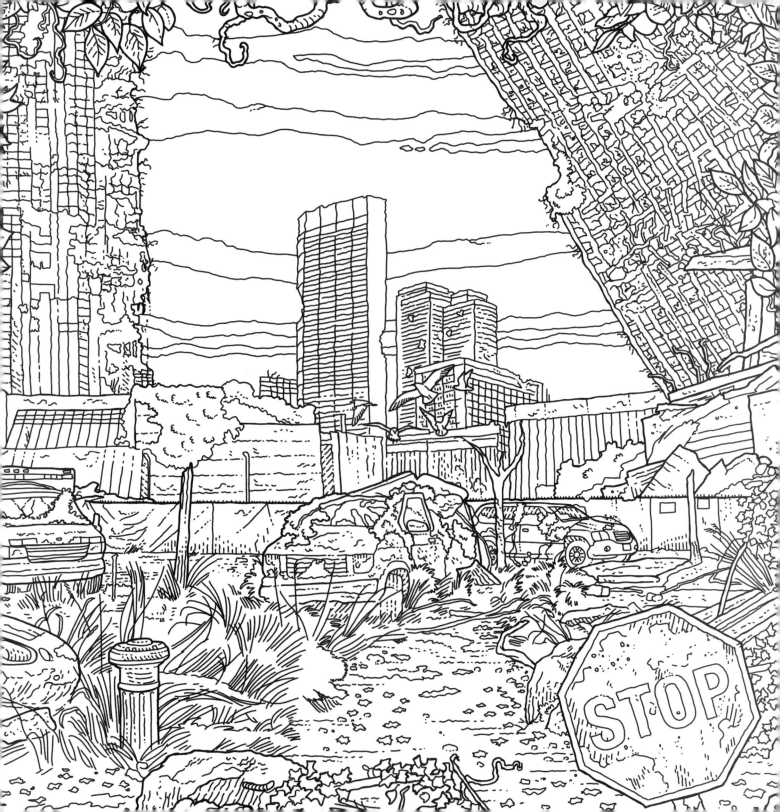

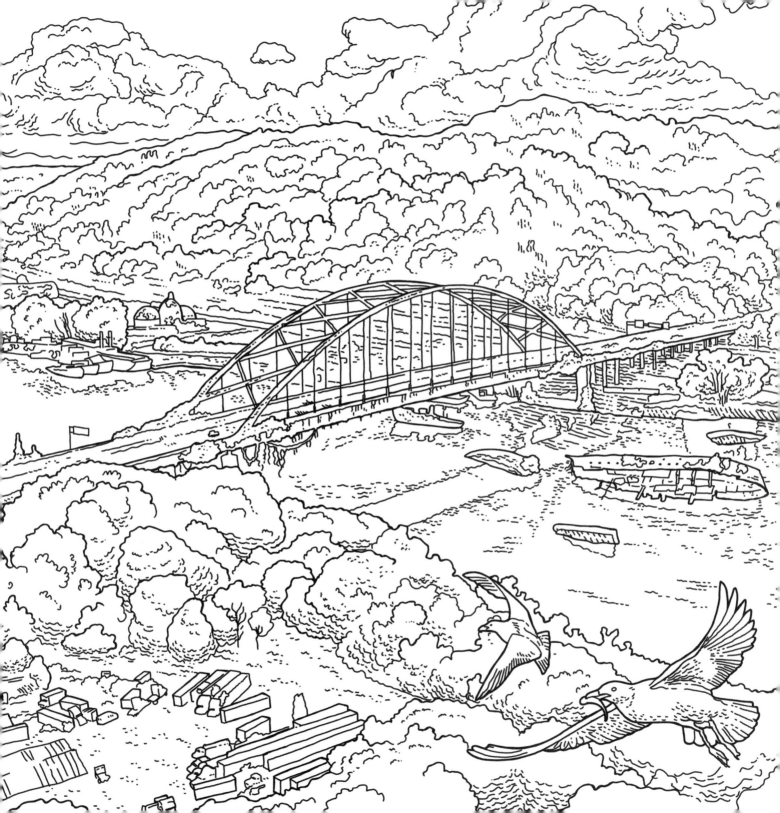

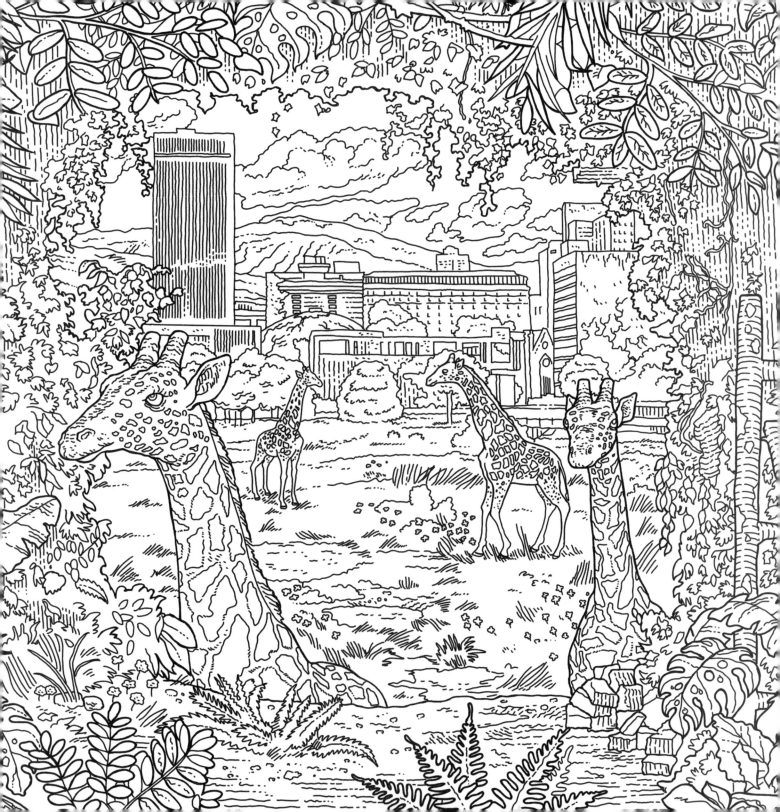

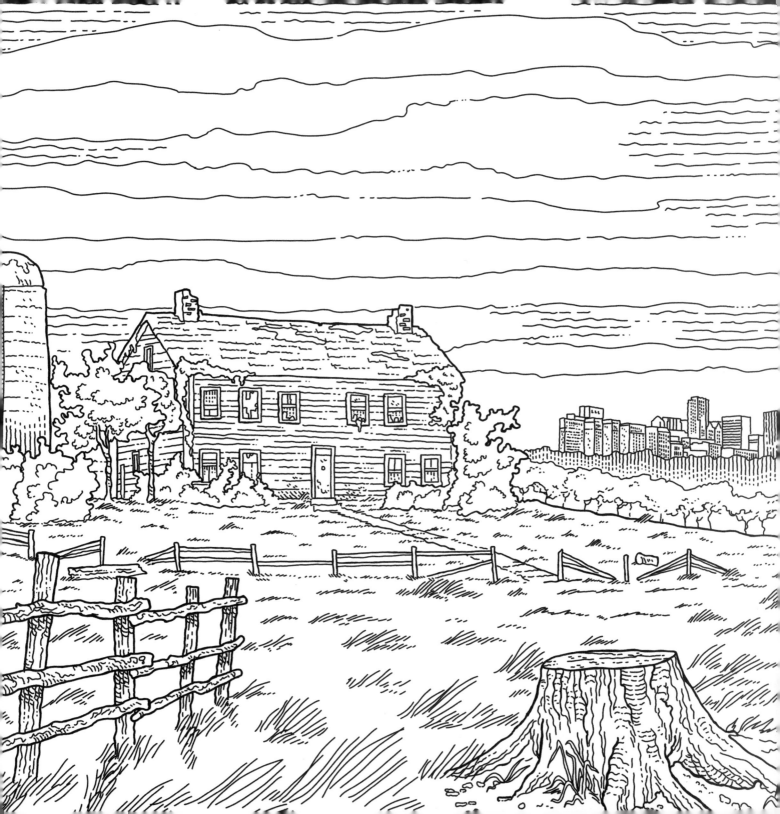

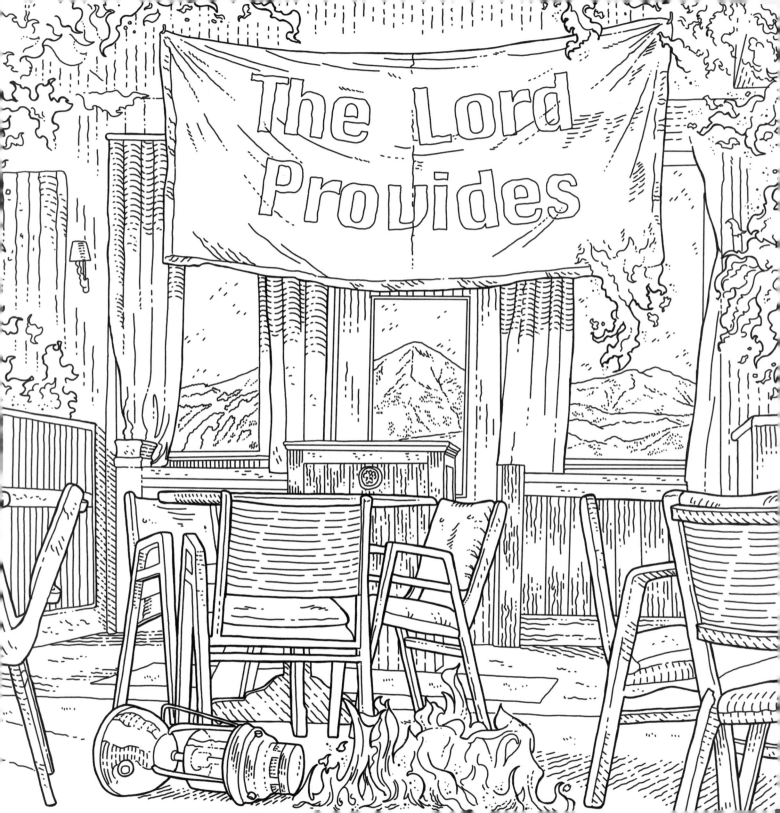

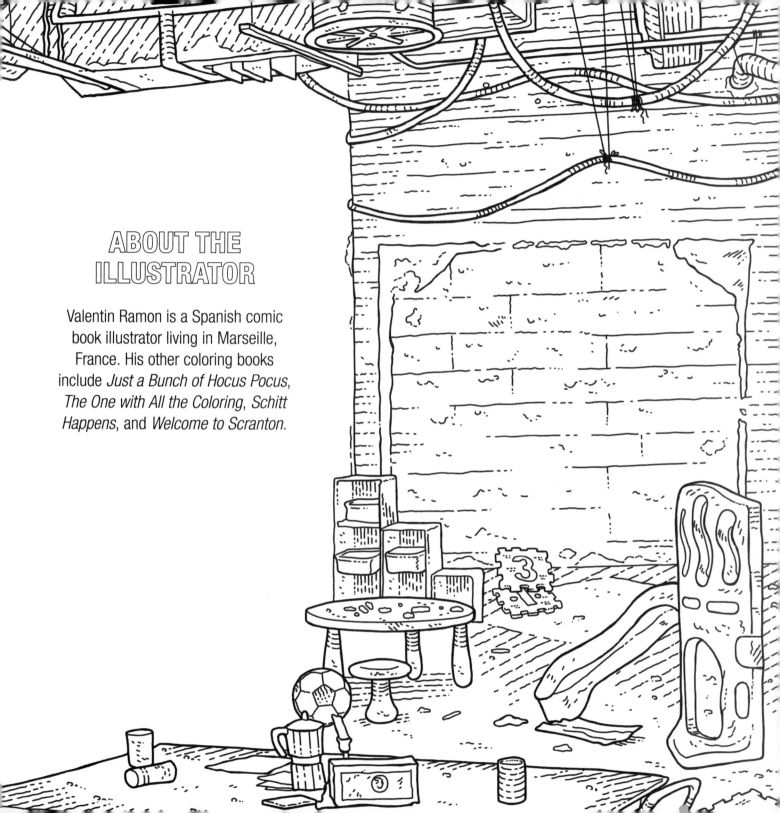

ABOUT THE ILLUSTRATOR

Valentin Ramon is a Spanish comic book illustrator living in Marseille, France. His other coloring books include *Just a Bunch of Hocus Pocus*, *The One with All the Coloring*, *Schitt Happens*, and *Welcome to Scranton*.

DISCOVER MORE GREAT COLORING BOOKS
FROM ULYSSES PRESS

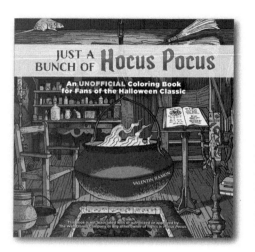

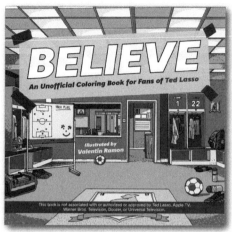

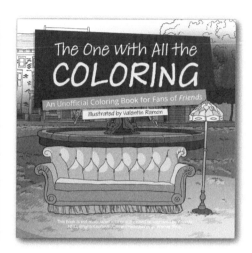

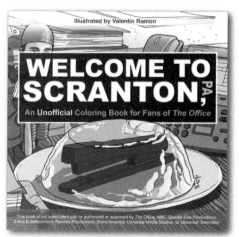

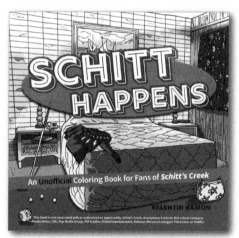

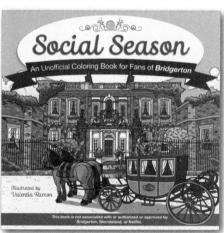

www.ulyssespress.com/coloring